The Ten Commandments for Teaching

The Author

Ray Reyes is a Business Teacher at Parlier High School, California.

The Advisory Panel

Patrick J. Devine, Mathematics Teacher, Chaparral Junior High School, Alamogordo, New Mexico

Troy Field, English and Social Studies Teacher, Browerville High School, Minnesota

Barry W. Thomas, Classroom Teacher, Baltimore County Schools; Instructor, Carroll Community College, Maryland

Carol A. Weiss, English Teacher, West Scranton High School, Scranton, Pennsylvania

The Ten Commandments for Teaching:

A Teacher's View

by Ray Reyes

Reference & Resource Series

nea PROFESSIONAL LIBRARY
National Education Association
Washington, D.C.

Copyright © 1991
National Education Association of the United States

Printing History
   First Printing: October 1991

Note
The opinions expressed in this publication should not be construed as representing the policy or position of the National Education Association. Materials published by the NEA Professional Library are intended to be discussion documents for teachers who are concerned with specialized interests of the profession.

Library of Congress Cataloging-in-Publication Data

Reyes, Raymond Steven, 1950-
    The ten commandments for teaching: a teacher's view/by Ray Reyes.
       p.   cm.—(Reference & resource series)
    Includes bibliographical references.
    ISBN 0-8106-1539-8
    1. Teaching. 2. Learning, Psychology of. 3. Teacher-student
relationships. 4. Education—Philosophy. I. National Education
Association of the United States. II. Title. III. Series:
Reference and resource series.
LB1025.3.R49 1991
371.1'02—dc20   90-27162
                                                        CIP

CONTENTS

PREFACE

It was August 1981 and I was in the second week of midlevel management training in Chicago. I remember looking around the room and realizing that I was the youngest person there. My career had been fruitful and I had even begun envisioning myself in the highest executive positions of the Internal Revenue Service. That day we were to meet one of the bright young stars of the executive ranks.

His presentation had a mesmerizing effect on me, but in a manner I had never dreamed possible. The more I listened to him talk, the more I saw myself sitting in his place—but I didn't like what I saw. He was brash and cocky, definitely committed to his job. That wasn't my concern. What bothered me was that I never heard him talk about the human side of his job. I never sensed that he really understood how important his employees were in accomplishing his very ambitious goals. I didn't care for the image he projected as a leader in the organization.

Was this how people in the organization would perceive me in the future? Would I really be able to make a difference? Or would the organization swallow up my management creativity and transform my style into the status quo? Would I have to become less people-oriented in order to progress into the executive ranks? I thought about it that night.

The following morning during the next segment it hit me. Deep down inside I had always wanted to be a teacher. The presentation the day before had taken me into the future. It made me project myself and my career into the next 5 to 10 years. How did I want to spend the rest of my working life? I was always aware that there was a teacher inside me waiting to escape, but career success had overshadowed the urge. Being away from my job and family for two weeks gave me time to think about my direction in life. But I quickly made up my mind. I was going to teach.

The decision was easy to make but making it happen was considerably more complex. My wife was not working. We had just welcomed our fourth child a few months before. I was making $40,000 annually and first-year teachers were earning $15,000. My wife didn't find my decision amusing. In fact, she thought I was nuts. It took her a year to get over the shock. But being the loyal, loving wife that she is, she went right back to work to help me realize my dream.

In August 1985 I walked into the classroom for the first time. My professional and personal life hasn't been the same since. I knew immediately that I had done the right thing. I realized that I was a teacher who hadn't been teaching. But that was all over now. Confucius is credited with saying, "Show me people who love their job, and I'll show you people who will never work a day in their lives." I know what he meant.

I look forward to my job and believe that all people can have the kind of enthusiasm for their careers. If you are now a teacher and this message hits home, this text will help you enjoy your job in ways that perhaps you forgot were possible. If you are planning to enter the teaching profession, I am certain that the following pages will provide you with some practical methods that will make your initial teaching experiences more rewarding. I also feel that the text is an easy reference for all of us. While many new teachers drown in their first three years, experienced teachers (and other professionals) often become stale and begin going through the motions. Everyone can benefit from periods of rejuvenation. I hope that the contents of these pages can be helpful in both situations.

The first nine commandments are quick, easy reading, directly related to teaching. The Tenth Commandment comprises the key portion of this publication. It will help you execute the first nine commandments. This last commandment also addresses your personal life because, for most of us, it is tightly interwoven with our careers. If you read the text, think about it, and practice its principles, I guarantee it will change your life for the better.

Veterans of the teaching profession will find no new and revolutionary teaching methods or philosophies; they will discover good food for thought. I wrote this text with three purposes in mind: (1) to help make you a better teacher; (2) to help you enjoy your job and life more; and (3) to serve as an ongoing source of teaching fundamentals, benefiting aspiring teachers, as well as those who periodically feel something is missing from their day-to-day teaching. Let me share an experience that emphasizes this third point. It was instrumental in convincing me that this publication could be extremely useful in our profession. In 1987, I was the football coach when our school faced an important game. If we lost we would not qualify for the playoffs. The opposing team was in first place and had allowed only one touchdown in five games. About a week before the game, one of my coaching peers called to wish me luck. We had played and beaten his team a few weeks earlier. During the course of the conversation he kept mentioning how much trouble his players had finding the ball when they played us. He said that our ball handling was so good that on many occasions his players were chasing a player *who did not have the ball.*

After I hung up the phone I realized that in the three weeks since that game, our team had become less and less effective because we had become less and less deceptive, the very thing my coach friend told me was one of our *greatest assets.* That week, we reemphasized that part of our game, scored 23 points, won the game, and made the playoffs.

My analogy is this. Many times in the classroom we stray from the very things that make us effective. These methods or strategies are so fundamental, so elementary, yet, over a period of days, weeks, or months, we forget how important they are. This text may give you some new ideas. For veteran teachers, however, it is more likely to reinforce some good, sound teaching methods that just need to be reemphasized.

There is something else you should know about the development of *The Ten Commandments for Teaching*. It suggests teaching methods that are student-centered. That is, it addresses the most common concerns of students about teachers. Many times I will refer to feedback received from students, which was compiled from written questionnaires over a period of three years. In seeking input about what students felt made a teacher effective or ineffective, I have attempted to mesh modern educational teaching theory with practical suggestions in order to identify the attributes that make a teacher exceptional.

I mention this student-centered foundation because I know that some educators do not feel students can provide valid criticism of our profession. I respect their right to disregard student perceptions. *The Ten Commandments for Teaching* will be of little value to people who feel this way. I also could not disagree with this view more. I believe students *do* know what sound teaching practices are and their input can be extremely helpful in the most essential task of educating our country's youth.

The First Commandment

THOU SHALT REMEMBER THAT WE'RE IN IT FOR THE CHILDREN

There must exist an underlying premise for all professions. People of the cloth, for example, possess a concern for the spiritual development of their congregations. They usually care a great deal for the humans whose lives they touch. Theirs is a people-oriented commitment.

All of us should choose our careers with a set of goals in mind. Some of these goals are material-related, intended to take care of our lifestyle desires or obligations. Other goals are people-oriented, with a humanistic purpose of primary importance. Teaching always has been and hopefully always will be a highly people-oriented profession. This is the unwritten and unstated creed of the teaching profession. I believe that one must care a great deal about children to achieve excellence in our profession.

Many teachers underestimate the impact they have on students. At our best we can turn students on. Unfortunately, when we are not at our best, we can turn them off. We possess that kind of power.

A veteran teacher once referred to what she called the Bermuda Triangle of education. The triangle is comprised of the parent, the child, and the teacher. When all three are committed to the educational process, it is the best possible opportunity for learning to flourish. The absence of any one of the triangle components obviously complicates matters considerably. A broken home usually affects the triangle adversely; so does the student who lacks motivation. But, *teachers must remain the constant*. We must always be there. The student must always be able to count on us. There can be no excuses for it being any other way. It is our job.

Perhaps one of teaching's greatest challenges is forging this three-pronged cooperative team. It is more difficult as multicultural classrooms are emerging nationwide. Language and cultural barriers often inhibit the development of a good cooperative relationship between parent, student, and teacher. Establishing this triangle often will require nothing short of an extraordinary effort by the teacher. But the rewards are great. A team of three will always be more successful in the long run because student, parent, and teacher accountability is enhanced.

A common complaint heard from teachers is that parents don't care about their children's education. This is as much a myth as what some parents say about teachers. Stereotyping or generalizing by teachers or parents does not show good judgment and often many of us begin believing the myths we are perpetuating. The vast majority of students I have talked to (and I work in the poorest community in California) say their parents do care about their education. Maybe their parents don't care as much as we think they should, but they do care. In any event, as classroom instructors we have little control over this and should direct our energies toward maximizing classroom learning.

Remember: We're in it for the children; don't underestimate the impact you have on your students. An illustration of the second point—my first grade daughter brought home her oral assignment listing four things she loved. Her teacher was *first*. I was *fourth*, listed after Mom and the cat.

The Second Commandment

THOU SHALT REMEMBER THAT DISCIPLINE PRECEDES LEARNING

Sometimes the most obvious concept is the first forgotten. Most problems in classroom teaching are related to the lack of discipline. A former teacher of mine estimated that most teachers leave the profession due to their inability to control their classrooms. Many also agree that most incoming teachers don't realize how critical discipline is. In fact, *discipline*, in my opinion, *precedes learning*. You cannot teach without first establishing classroom control.

Discipline is a key concept in our lives and must be present to regularly succeed at anything. As a football coach, I must have discipline. I must make clear what my rules are and what the consequences are if the rules are not followed. I practice what I preach when I enforce the rules. The rules must apply to everyone, especially to superstars.

The same thing applies in the classroom. You must establish discipline first. What are your rules? What the consequences if a student does not follow them? Do you enforce the rules with everyone, even the superstars? You know the right answers to these questions, but how would your students answer these questions about you? Why don't you ask them? You might be surprised with their answers.

A major myth about students is that if you gave them the opportunity, they would create chaos in the classroom. The fact is, however, that most students want classroom discipline.

Before I decided to give up my management career and enter teaching, I asked my older sister, a teacher, if children were really different nowadays. I had heard so many horror stories after the unrest of the 1960s. My sister told me, "Yes, children are different, but it'll be easier for you because you're a man and football coach." I have now had five years to reflect on my sister's comments and I have two reactions.

First, I wholeheartedly agree: Children have changed. Do you know why? Because the adults have changed and the adults raised them. What did we expect? I began my management career in 1975. I wouldn't have lasted long had I used the same management style and techniques in the 1980s. People change and managers, coaches, parents, teachers, and anyone else who deals with people must likewise adapt in order to maintain effectiveness.

I realize that it is popular to say, "If it ain't [sic] broke, don't fix it." But I've seen too many capable managers, coaches, and others in people-intensive professions go under because they kept waiting for everyone else to change while the world passed them by. My point is this: We must be cognizant of the changes that are going on around us. They may require only subtle adjustments or no adjustment at all. But no one can argue with the need to adapt to the changes that take place in our lives.

My second reaction to my sister's comments has to do with classroom discipline being easier for men. It might be true that certain students will test women teachers more than they will men. But it was my experience that some of the best, most effective classroom control was exhibited by my female teachers. Good classroom management is the most important factor, *not* the sex of the instructor.

Here are some suggestions that will help you improve classroom control:

1. *Follow school discipline procedures.* It seems simple because it is. If your school has a disciplinary policy in place, follow it.

2. *Be strict until Turkey Day.* This is the well-known teacher axiom that suggests being very strict until Thanksgiving, then, if warranted, slacking off as the students show they deserve it.

Like anything else, it is easier to be strict at first and then loosen the reins, than to attempt to regain control after being too lenient.

3. *Use common sense and creativity.* It really bothers me when I hear teachers scream to get their students' attention. I have not yelled once to get attention in my classroom. (This is not to say I haven't felt like yelling.) Use seating charts to separate students who enjoy each other's company too much. Students themselves are almost always amazed how much more they learn without the temptation to talk to a friend. If you are lecturing and students are talking, walk over and stand near the talkers. Don't say a word, and watch what happens.

Many effective teachers use warm up or "sponge" activities that require students to start to work as soon as class begins. I know a teacher who uses the Two Minute Warning; when the bell rings, students are expected to be quietly working. The teacher deducts points from citizenship grades if students do not comply as expected. Once these procedures are established, students develop a good habit, which is just as hard to break as a bad habit. Students learn to come to class and get to work. This makes the teacher's job so much easier and leaves a positive impression with any visitors.

At the beginning of many class periods, I use dumb jokes to get students' attention. In fact, I have earned a reputation among students for telling stupid jokes. This is fine with me. Every time I start a joke in class I have the attention of every student (all of whom want to see how dumb my joke will be), which is exactly what I want. As soon as their reaction to the joke is finished, I slip right into my lecture or next lesson.

4. *Discipline uniformly and without malice.* The first way students identify your pets is the way you administer discipline. I cannot emphasize this point enough, so I'll do it again: Don't favor students over others, for *any* reason.

Also, it does little or no good to discipline a student with malice in your expression. Discipline calmly, even with a smile, and send the student off with, "I still love you, Melissa." There's no need to demonstrate anger. Anger, on the part of the teacher, usually only escalates the issue.

Also be ready for the argumentative student whom you have asked to sign a contract or documentation. Here are some of my favorite responses:

Johnny, I'm just doing my job and teaching you how to do yours.

Becky, you should see how I treat *my* kids!

If I didn't care about you, I'd let you come in late everyday.

ALMOST ALL CLASSROOM LEARNING DIFFI-CULTIES ARE RELATED TO THE LACK OF CLASS-ROOM CONTROL.

The Third Commandment

THOU SHALT DEMONSTRATE THE RELEVANCY OF LEARNING

Have you ever found yourself doing something with no purpose? Most of us would answer no, but we probably have. What is certain is that almost all of us would not consciously do something for no apparent reason. Yet, many times, as teachers we seemingly ask or expect our students to learn just for the sake of learning.

Learning is a delayed gratification process; we work for payoff in the future. A certain percentage of children understand the importance of maintaining a competitive grade point average, know the benefit of taking a rigorous schedule of courses, and, in general, are self-disciplined enough to take their studies seriously.

On the other hand, there are numerous other students (and I was one of them) who are not sure what their career paths are going to be, and/or who have not given much thought to the value or importance of their studies. It is my contention that the more relevant the teacher makes the learning, the more benefit the student sees in it. I believe it would be safe to say that if all other things were equal, the student who sees the practical benefits from or the relevancy of their studies to their needs will put forth a more concerted effort. We should remember this and be prepared when students ask us, "Why am I studying this?"

As teachers, we must be able to show how the pieces fit into the big puzzle. How will learning this particular subject directly or indirectly benefit the student? We must help students improve their learning by grasping the subject matter holistically. Students should comprehend the individual components of learning, as well as the way the components fit together in the entire process.

Let me give you an example. When I was an undergraduate, my advisors expressed surprise that my grade point average was not higher. One specifically suggested that I improve my grades, but I never really understood why. I assumed it was the normal pep talk I had always heard about grades. Later, however, I found out why when I applied for graduate work. The grade point average was an important factor in gaining acceptance into the master's program. You can be sure that if someone had told me *why* it was important to improve my grade point average, it would have had a much bigger impact on me. But, no one told me and I was too ignorant to ask. I believe my advisors were well intentioned but assumed I knew the reason.

Here are some suggestions for demonstrating the relevancy of learning:

1. *Periodically review the learning that has taken place.* This shows students the progress they have made and also allows you to integrate previous learning with current subject matter.

2. *Link learning to real life situations.* Use newspapers, magazines, and other methods to show the importance of subject matter.

3. *If you teach single subject matter, don't limit your demonstrations of relevancy to your area of expertise.* For example, the business teacher at a high school can read the classified advertisements every day and show how good typing skills can lead to immediate employment.

I've always felt that math teachers, in particular, would benefit greatly by demonstrating the relevancy of their subject. In fact, it is not uncommon to overhear students say "Why do we need to know quadratic equations, graphs, etc.?" Many of us can probably relate to these feelings.

In going through the classified section, one day I found an advertisement outlining the minimum requirements for apprentice electricians. One requirement caught my eye: Two years of high school algebra with a C grade or better. I read this to my students to show the importance of the math curriculum and to emphasize the importance and difference between a C and a D grade.

REMEMBER: FIND DIFFERENT WAYS TO AN-SWER THE "WHY?" QUESTION. Help students see what's in it for them.

The Fourth Commandment

THOU SHALT DANGLE THE CARROT HIGH

Almost every book I've read about human potential has indicated that psychologists agree that average human beings perform at approximately 15 percent of their brain potential. Students I surveyed, when asked "How much do average high school students put out compared to their full potential?" answered an amazingly consistent 15-25 percent. In other words, students agree with psychologists: We are all capable of much more than we are currently achieving.

Look at it this way. If we teachers are performing at 15 percent of our potential and motivating students is one of the most important aspect of the job, we should be able to motivate our students *at least twice as effectively as we do currently*. I know that this sounds like an old cliché, but we need to drive this message home. We need to push students into doubling their efforts and to work hard for their own good. Teachers must constantly challenge students. *No ifs, ands, or buts!*

The issue of high expectations is a critical one. The remarkable exploits of mathematics teacher Jaime Escalante at Garfield High School in Los Angeles are a good example. Teachers cannot fall prey to stereotypical expectation setting because they have economically or educationally disadvantaged students. Lower teacher expectations only perpetuate the cycle of underachievement for these students.

A careful balance must be struck. Unrealistically high expectations can lead to student and teacher frustration, but low expectations limit intellectual development and ultimately become far more costly for society. I believe high expectations are most important for traditionally lower-achieving segments of our multicultural student population. This philosophy was at the root of Escalante's success.

Don't allow students to con themselves with success-stopping phrases such as, "I don't know" or "I can't," or shrug their shoulders. These responses are not allowed in my classroom. Once students learn that they are able to deflect a teacher's question to another student by using one of these success-stopping phrases, the teacher has given them an escape clause. Students lose their incentive to pay attention in class when they learn they can weasel out of the question in this manner. Consequently, all my students are expected to answer—or at a minimum, make a legitimate effort to answer—the teacher's question. They learn quickly that they will not be let off the hook. I believe students are more likely to pay attention when they know a question could be directed at them and, more importantly, that they must respond.

An interesting event that occurred in my classroom illustrates the concept of *Dangling the Carrot High*. One day I came into my class and wrote the name of our high school on the chalkboard. I told students that they had five minutes to write as many words as they could using combinations of the school's letters. I gave small awards to the two students with the most words. My top student came up with 18 words, second place had 16 words, five students had 12 to 16 words, and the remaining 13 students had 8 to 12 words. Later that day when my other typing class came in, I gave them the same assignment with a slight twist. I told the class that every student in the earlier class finished *with at least 14 words*. (Now you know I tell little white lies.) When the second class finished, all but three students came up with 14 words or more. Dangling the carrot high significantly affected the results of the second class. The setting of a goal (14 words) gave students something to focus on. If the target is realistic, students will usually increase their effort and their performance.

The concept of goal setting is very important. Use yourself as an example. I know very few people who are successful

21

by accident. On the contrary, successful people use or have used goals as their main means of providing direction in their lives. Goal setting, which I will discuss again in the Tenth Commandment, whether short range (I want to get a B on my next algebra test) or long range (I want to become a teacher after I graduate from high school), is an extremely helpful tool in the classroom.

I have found two schools of practice regarding motivation of students. The first practice I call the "college professor" or "treat-'em-as-adults" method. Using this approach, students are told, "If you don't want to come to class or do your work, I'll give you the grade you deserve." Some teachers use the logic that students won't get babied in college, so why spoil them? They have to learn they are only cheating themselves. The underlying philosophy of this teaching concept is that students must learn to develop self-discipline, because if they don't they'll eventually fail somewhere down the line. I've talked to students who agree that this philosophy works very well, but only with those who are *self-motivated*.

What percentage of our students, however, are truly self-motivated? This is where the second practice comes in, the one that I observe. I call it "I'm going to treat you as I would my own child." I'm going to (figuratively) push, shove, scratch, kick, bite, call your parents, assign detention, send you to the dean—*whatever it takes* to make you see the light. Even if I know the student may get angry over my methods, I try to find the right chain to yank until I get her or him to realize what kind of effort is necessary. My goal is to help students discover what they are capable of when they put their mind to something.

STUDENT SURVEY RESULTS INDICATE THAT MANY STUDENTS EXPECT THEIR TEACHERS TO INSPIRE OR MOTIVATE THEM. MANY TEACHERS EXPECT THEIR STUDENTS TO ARRIVE SELF-MOTI-

VATED. COULD IT BE THAT WE'VE LOST STUDENTS BECAUSE BOTH TEACHERS AND STUDENTS HAVE BEEN SITTING BACK WAITING FOR MOTIVATION TO MAGICALLY ENGULF THE CLASSROOM?

The Fifth Commandment

THOU SHALT REMEMBER THAT PRECIOUS STONES COME FROM THE MOST UNLIKELY ROCKS

In every classroom, elementary through high school, there exists a small group of students who, over the course of months, even years, become faceless. Years from now it will be difficult, if not impossible, for any former teacher to recall much about these students. Whether we want to admit it or not, most of us are drawn to the student with the outgoing personality, the high achiever, and even the one who requires constant discipline. But in between these students are others who become faceless. They can be, and often are, forgotten.

If we, as teachers, assume that every student is capable of unlimited success, then we must make an extra effort to keep in touch with these students. It is easy to communicate with young people who have pleasing personalities. The problem is that they probably don't need the attention nearly as much as the faceless students who sit in class, never cause any problems, and may or may not excel academically. Nonetheless, we must take the initiative to make these students feel at home, to feel wanted, to feel like part of the group, because we never really know which students will ultimately develop into precious stones.

In order to avoid overlooking potential precious stones, I suggest following these simple guidelines:

1. *Don't run the T formation.* Most observers say that many teachers wear out the classroom floor with a path across the front of the room and down the middle aisle. This kind of classroom movement limits contact with students. It creates an actual physical separation, which surely cannot be as effective as

maintaining closer physical proximity to them. And those faceless students who bury themselves in the back corners of the classroom may not come within 20–30 feet of a teacher all day. This is sad. Effective teachers do not allow this to happen.

A colleague once told me that every child has a lock, which when unlocked, opens the student up to the teacher and increases the likelihood of improved learning. Effective teachers look for and find the keys that open these locks.

This reminds me of the deadpan-faced student who transferred into my class during the middle of the school year. She was obviously not thrilled about the development. For weeks I made numerous attempts to get her to crack a smile, laugh, or even respond to me with more than a nod of the head. One day I mentioned that my wife had graduated from the school from which she had transferred. Her face lit up immediately. I had found the key. Once we discovered that common strand, or the one thing she could relate to, she became much more responsive academically.

2. *Show interest in all your students.* Whenever you involve your students with jobs in the classroom, don't forget anyone. I think that elementary teachers are much better at this than secondary teachers. Involve as many students as you can. For example, I have a list of my students' birthdays. I keep these posted on a calendar and I write each student a short, personal note wishing her or him a happy birthday. Although secondary teachers often see this as more of an elementary school practice, I can assure you that high school students appreciate the recognition, and it pays big dividends in improving student/ teacher relationships.

3. *Remember the slogan "Reach out and touch someone."* Maintain a personal touch with all your students. If you and your students start off the day or class period on the right foot, it sets the tone for the balance of the instructional time. A salutation or compliment to each student is a small price to pay and reaps tremendous benefits in establishing and maintaining a harmoni-

ous classroom environment.

DON'T FORGET, IF STUDENTS WIN, YOU WIN!

The Sixth Commandment

THOU SHALT REMEMBER THAT THE LITTLE THINGS MAKE A BIG DIFFERENCE

In the previous chapters, I have talked about many things that, if you commit to them, will allow you to distinguish yourself as a classroom teacher. Primarily, I have been addressing dynamics that contribute to a classroom climate that is more conducive to learning. If the climate of an organization is good—individuals are on task, expectations are understood, and most feel committed to the organization's goals—it is difficult *not* to be excellent. The same is true in the confines of our classrooms. We must strive for a climate, an energy, that is part of the class. The goal is to have students look forward to our class.

The three major components of climate are the classroom, the teacher, and the learning process itself. The classroom should be comfortable, neat, and organized. The teacher should be perceived as caring and genuinely concerned with students' education. The learning process must be disciplined (see the Second Commandment) and structured.

Teachers are an amazingly flexible group. This is best evidenced by the various work environments in which they operate. There are single-unit bungalows, large multipurpose rooms, rooms with poor acoustics, and many other less-than-desirable situations. While teachers sometimes have only limited control of their actual working environment, it is imperative that whatever we end up with, we make the most of it. Keeping this in mind, I have seen some teachers do fantastic things, with their bulletin boards, for example. Creative teachers can turn a drab environment into colorful, positive surroundings. Some teachers take pictures of students around campus or at school functions and post the pictures on classroom walls. I keep my "brag wall" where I post notes, cards, and presents I've received from appreciative students. Posters, bumper stickers, signs with motivational sayings, school logos, and positive analogies to the learning process contribute to the desired classroom environment.

The next time you walk into your room ask yourself these questions: Are the desks clean and neatly arranged? Is the room tidy? A consultant friend once told me he booked the managers of an organization into a room without checking it out in advance. The purpose of the meeting was to build teamwork and clear the air between people who were not working well together. The consultant termed the meeting results dismal. He felt the repressive environment of the room (no windows, bare walls, poor circulation) was a major contributing factor to the outcome of the meeting. This can, and does, happen in the educational setting as well. Teachers must transform poor environments into positive ones to enhance the learning process.

The second and third elements of the climate, the teacher and the learning process, are the most critical ingredients in determining the learning environment. If everything else is substandard, an effective teacher can, of course, more than compensate for it. Here are a few recommendations for enhancing classroom environment:

1. *Say something to every student every day.* This sounds so trivial and simple that you would be shocked at the number of teachers who don't even think about doing it. I once interviewed a group of employees who had worked in my organization for four months. In an interview before their layoff because of lack of work, I asked them to list the characteristics of a good supervisor. The top two responses were: "A good supervisor says 'Good morning' to you every day," and "A good supervisor knows your name." I found the responses incredible. I shared these

comments with my managers and we all agreed that we had all forgotten a *very little thing* that obviously *made a big difference.*

This suggestion can apply to teachers as well. Wait at the entrance of your classroom, armed with two very inexpensive tools: a compliment or a hello and a smile. There are literally millions of things you can say to students to make them welcome. Convince them consciously or unconsciously that you are glad to see them.

2. *Get to know your students.* The more you know about your students, the better job you can do assisting them to perform at full potential. I once learned that a student from a single-parent home was better motivated to solve a tardiness problem when I called his uncle. I picked up this information from a short questionnaire I give all students at the beginning of the year. In answer to the question "Who is the person you respect most?" he listed his uncle. When I attempted to change his behavior through his mother, I got no results. Shortly after contacting his uncle, he was on time to my class for the rest of the school year.

My student questionnaire includes the student's name, birth date, parents' names, addresses, home and work phone numbers, birth date, and other potentially important information. I also ask students their favorite football team colors, music group, etc. I use this information when I need an idea to reward or plan a strategy for motivating the student.

You can also use such questionnaire information to contact the home or call guardians with a student progress report. It saves time because you have all the information at your fingertips. A note of caution: Please don't send home only bad news. Your reputation as a teacher is greatly enhanced by regular and fair communication with the parent(s)—containing both good and bad news.

3. *Relate to students and their interests.* Many adults, including some teachers, tend to reject student lifestyles and fads. What are we telling students when we do this? Aren't we, at least,

rejecting a part of themselves? An awareness of your students' idols, favorite slang expressions, and movie stars, etc., shows an interest in the students and, perhaps more importantly, an acceptance of their tastes and opinions. Teachers who are accepted as "cool" have been identified by students as those who can communicate effectively with them. This can also help the teacher develop a productive learning environment.

4. *Bombard your students with positive reinforcement.* Drawing happy faces on papers will never outlive its usefulness. Don't stop doing it. Even at the high school level I still use "scratch n' sniff" stickers. The students love them. I've even had the biggest football players take me to task because I gave stickers only to the girls. Now I'm an equal opportunity sticker giver.

One teacher told me that she refuses to use red ink because children are tired of seeing it on corrected work. She now uses hot pinks, lavender, and other less offensive colors. I think she has a good point; her methods show that she is aware that little things make a big difference.

DON'T TAKE THE LITTLE THINGS FOR GRANTED.

The Seventh Commandment

THOU SHALT ERASE ALL QUESTION MARKS THOROUGHLY

In student surveys, by far the number one response to the open-ended question "An effective teacher. . ." was *explains the lessons properly.* To our students it was, without a doubt, the most important characteristic of good teaching—and it makes sense.

In response to the statement, "An ineffective teacher. . .", the converse was true. Students responded that ineffective teachers' most significant shortcoming was not adequately explaining new lessons or materials. Put yourself into your students' shoes. Any of us can relate to taking a course in high school or college and feeling frustrated because we are not grasping the content. We look to the teacher to lead us out of our state of confusion. Almost always our perception of a "good" teacher is based on the ability to "erase our question marks" about the subject matter. I think it is safe to say that students use our ability to explain lessons clearly as the primary means to determine our effectiveness as instructors.

A major complaint about teachers is that we "get mad" when students ask questions. As one student wrote: "One thing that turns me off as a student is when the teacher is showing you something on the board, you ask a question, and the teacher gets mad saying you should have paid attention. I *was* paying attention. I just got lost." Now if we think about it, how do we feel when someone erroneously accuses us of something? I venture to say that we lose a little respect for that individual. When teachers lose even a little of the respect of their students, the learning process is adversely affected until that respect is regained.

The problem with getting mad when asked a question by a student is that it cuts off future student questions. Children are not stupid; if they hear a peer ask the teacher a question and get an angry reply, how anxious do you think they will be to subject themselves to similar treatment? A teacher once told me that he felt the "1 + 5 Rule" was true for the majority of questions asked in the classroom. According to this rule, for every student who asks you a question, there are five other students who wanted to ask the same question but are afraid of appearing stupid to their peers.

Let's look at the teacher's side for a minute. Why do teachers get upset when a student asks a question? I think there are two major reasons. The first reason is that sometimes the children are just not paying attention. As the father of a right-brained child, I can relate to this. My oldest son is probably often taking grand mental journeys into outer space or visualizing himself conquering the latest Nintendo game. Similar situations occur in the classroom all the time. Daydreaming, short attention spans, and other deterrents are part of the hand you're dealt as a teacher. Get used to it! It's entirely possible that one of your students has just received a first kiss and is mentally in the arms of that girlfriend or boyfriend. How well do you think the student will be listening to you? Then, of course, there is the student who has legitimate family or personal problems. Mix all these students together and you probably have a fairly typical classroom. This is the teacher's challenge.

To combat this kind of environment calls for creativity and, as students like to say, being "off the wall." This calls for the use of attention getters. Try speaking with an accent (Southern, French, New York, etc.) and watch the reactions of your students. Zero in on your daydreamers by asking them the lion's share of the questions as you go through the lesson. This is a subtle way of letting them know they must be on their toes in your class. If the class seems dead, burnt out (most commonly known as post-lunch syndrome), or otherwise listless, have students stand, get in lines, and give each other neck rubs. This takes two or three minutes but does wonders for invigorating the class. Also walk around the classroom, especially near students who appear to need your attention. Talk louder. Whisper. There are many things you can do to get attention—you are limited only by your imagination.

The second, and most interesting, reason teachers get upset when asked questions is this: We take it personally. For example, we have just given an enthusiastic lecture and a student raises a hand and says, "I don't get it! We then quickly go to the student's rescue with a couple of clarifying statements. The student's face obviously shows that your great explanation didn't do the job. You're sure this is the case when the student says, "I still don't understand!" What many of us do at this juncture is predictable. We usually make a comment like, "It's really easy, you just. . ." Of course, it's easy. For us it is easy! We've been studying or teaching the subject for years. Therefore we take it personally because each time the student doesn't understand and tells us so, we seem to hear "You're not explaining it very well, teacher." When this occurs we become frustrated because we know that transferring knowledge from ourselves to our students is the major function of a teacher. However, when we let this frustration become anger—aimed at students who ask questions—it is counterproductive to our mission in the classroom.

Here are some suggestions to help you erase all question marks thoroughly:

1. *Give directions carefully.* Stress important points by repeating them or demonstrating them through analogies or practical hands-on applications.

2. *Constantly request feedback.* Continually request feedback from the class. "Are there any questions?" "Randy, is everything okay? Do you understand?" "Are you *sure?*" Also,

read the nonverbal cues on your students' faces; facial expressions rarely lie.

3. *Be patient.* Even when you feel like screaming, relax and remember this rule. When you think you have explained it enough, but you realize you haven't, be patient.

Several years ago in a workshop in our school district, Madeline Hunter, a proponent of the Clinical Teaching Model, compared teaching to a bus trip. As you start teaching a new lesson, she said, students get on the bus with you. Some students get on the bus before others.

DON'T LEAVE ANYONE AT THE BUS STOP. ERASE ALL QUESTION MARKS THOROUGHLY.

The Eighth Commandment

THOU SHALT REMEMBER THAT THE EXCEPTIONAL TEACHER IS ALWAYS LEARNING

During the past 20 years I have had an opportunity to meet, talk, and work with many people in a variety of professions. I did my master's work with top and midlevel managers from newspaper organizations, hospitals, private industry, and education. I was fortunate to interact with all these people and learn what made them tick. An important factor in the success of these individuals was and is their willingness to continually learn. They never seem to be satisfied with their performance and constantly challenge themselves to improve.

Because teaching is a crucial profession in our society, it is no different in terms of identifying those who ultimately excel. People at the top of their profession are always looking for the edge. They attend college classes and seminars; they read professional journals and articles; they watch television programs; they also talk with their peers in order to learn how to improve their professional performance. There are many ways, some conventional and some unconventional, to develop in your profession. It is a mistake to stand pat in any profession and assume your education is complete. A thirst for learning separates you from the rest of the pack.

More interesting, perhaps, is the perceptiveness of today's students. The following student comments address the importance of maintaining growth in our careers:

Some teachers never update their teaching methods. Every year it's obvious that their teaching patterns are repetitive. It bores you. They need to attend workshops and get new ideas.

35

Too often I have seen teachers use class time to assign work and not teach. They just sit at their desk.

I find this last comment profound. Students expect teachers to teach, to inspire, not assign work just to keep them busy. They seem to be saying, "Teach us!"

My suggestion for such teachers is, let your students evaluate your performance at the end of the school year. How you would do this depends on the grade level you teach.

Don't ask students to evaluate you, however, you are thick-skinned and can take constructive criticism. Remember you're asking for it. The student evaluation form in the Appendix addresses the areas most students feel are critical in determining a teacher's overall effectiveness (communication, fairness, grading system, the ability to explain things in an understandable way, and discipline).

Another important reason for teachers to constantly upgrade their skills relates to the change cycles in today's world which are becoming shorter and shorter each decade. For example, technology is impacting our lives in every way, including education. Demographics and societal norms are changing rapidly. Understanding the history and cultural traits of emerging ethnic groups takes extra effort. There is no doubt, however, that the culturally aware teacher is in a much better position to succeed. The need to assess the impact of these changes and their effect on our teaching methods and strategies will become even more critical as we enter the twenty-first century.

I truly believe that teachers will learn much about how they are perceived by their students if they ask for feedback in the key teaching areas. Moreover, they'll be better teachers if they take the feedback seriously.

The Ninth Commandment

THOU SHALT NOT UNDERESTIMATE THE POWER OF COMMUNICATION

Take everything away from a teacher—eliminate the books, classroom, computers, handouts. Even without all these necessities, the teacher who communicates effectively can and will teach. Communication is the *essence of teaching*. There is no more important tool for teachers than communication. They must be effective communicators.

The Third Commandment indicated the importance of demonstrating the relevancy of learning. I will attempt to practice what I preach by reviewing the classic Communication Model. To appreciate the power of communication, one should first understand the process of communication.

First of all, I have found the following definition of communication to be functional and simple to grasp. Communication is *the transmission of information from one source to another*. The first step of the communication process is the *idea* or *message*. Step two is the *sender* or *encoder* (the person or object that transmits the idea). Step three is the *medium* or manner in which the idea is sent. And the last step of the process is the *receiver* or *decoder* (the person(s) to whom the idea is being communicated).

Without getting unnecessarily complex, I think it is enough to say that once the idea has originated, the sender transmits it through any of a variety of media (verbal, nonverbal, written, electronic) to the receiver. This is an example of one-way communication. Potential problems include errors of omission (the sender leaves out some of the message), improper encoding (the sender miscommunicates the message), or the use of the wrong medium.

Another potential problem to effective communication occurs when interference blocks the message. Let me give you an example.

In my role as a consultant, I was once asked to help analyze the staff meetings of a critical part of the organization—a round-the-clock operation that relied heavily upon meetings between outgoing and incoming shifts to articulate work priorities. Management felt that the ball was being dropped too often between shifts due to misunderstandings or miscommunication during these daily meetings. While attending six meetings in two days, I was annoyed by an air conditioning fan in the meeting place, which made it very difficult to hear people who had their backs to me. After one of the meetings I asked a manager if she could hear everything that was being communicated. Her reply was, "No, we've told them we can't hear in this room!" Needless to say, a new, more appropriate meeting place was soon found.

If you have broken the Second Commandment ("Discipline Precedes Learning"), then you probably have firsthand knowledge of how the interference of classroom noise or disruptions stifles communication of your educational message. One time when I was asked to fill in for an absent colleague, I found myself continually interrupted by screaming youngsters from the nearby elementary school. Later I asked the teacher if this was a common occurrence. He answered, "All the time."

I think we are negligent if we don't insist on a quiet, learning atmosphere. If the interference comes from a source outside our control, then it becomes our responsibility to notify our administrators that the condition exists and ask for their help in resolving the situation. We must be persistent in our quest to provide students with the appropriate learning environment.

The communication model example outlined earlier is an example of one-way communication. Most communication is one-way or two-way. Effective teachers predominantly use two-way communication in their classrooms because it is inherently superior to one-way communication. Let me elaborate.

In the communication model I discussed the communication of a message from sender to receiver. The discussion did not mention the *feedback loop*. This loop is a necessary part of the communication process when the receiver doesn't understand the message. In such cases, the receiver will communicate back to the sender requesting clarification. If the teacher encourages two-way communication in the classroom, students will raise their hands and give the teacher (sender) *feedback* that the message was not understood. The teacher (sender) then recommunicates until students (receivers) do understand. All teachers will recognize this as a very common classroom procedure. What we must understand is that it is not only very common, but it is also extremely *crucial*. As I mentioned in the Seventh Commandment ("Thou Shalt Erase All Question Marks"), getting upset or angry with student questions will eventually cut off your feedback. This feedback is critical to teachers because it notifies us when students need clarification or when they just don't understand. Without this feedback, where are we?

The power of communication is also vitally important in establishing a good rapport with the parents of students. Chapter 2 discussed the Bermuda Triangle of education. Few can argue that the ideal conditions for learning are the result of a good working relationship between student, parent, and teacher. With the dramatic increase of non-English-speaking students in many of our schools, communication between teachers and parents has been cut off. Here, especially, the ability to maintain open communication channels is vital. The use of bilingual skills, interpreters, or bilingual aides are among the better methods of ensuring communication between the teacher and the home in these instances. Students perform best when they are held accountable. Accountability comes when the student knows the teacher and the parent have prompt access (communication) to each other.

Another aspect of communication is the importance of nonverbal communication. Remember that both teacher and students are continually communicating nonverbally. Our faces (expressions) rarely lie. "Confusion can easily be detected on student faces, for example. Teachers at the top of their profession know when their lesson has not hit home.

Here are some suggestions for increasing your effectiveness as a communicator:

1. *Accept only a verbal yes from students when asking if they understand new subject matter. Don't assume they understand.* I discussed this in the Seventh Commandment, but it needs to be stressed.

2. *Use effective methods to get students' attention.* Since there are approximately 180 days in a school year and secondary students walk into at least six different classes a day, there is a need to motivate students *to listen*. Again, a sense of humor, reading short articles of high interest to students, being off the wall, or other methods of getting attention are extremely effective in initiating the learning process.

Earlier, I mentioned my attention getters: speaking with accents, talking like an intellectual, or a teenager, and a variety of weird role plays. My objective in all cases is to get students' attention. In other words, I use these techniques as my handle or lead-in to a lesson.

I'm sure many teachers will say "I don't think I should have to resort to such tactics." I agree. If you're like me and feel comfortable acting off the wall, have fun with it. But if the shoe doesn't fit, for goodness sake, don't wear it. There are many, more conventional ways of maintaining students' attention and hundreds more that no one has thought of yet.

3. *Remember to increase two-way communication in the classroom.* You do this by encouraging questions, communicat-

ing effectively both verbally and nonverbally, and reading the nonverbal feedback from your students' faces.

The Tenth Commandment

THOU SHALT REMEMBER THAT A POSITIVE ATTITUDE IS YOUR MOST IMPORTANT POSSESSION

The first nine commandments have covered the fundamental elements of teaching excellence, but the Tenth Commandment is the ingredient that makes everything work. If the first nine commandments are the bricks with which to build exceptional teaching skills, then the Tenth Commandment is the mortar that bonds the bricks. To be honest, I feel you must practice the Tenth Commandment in order to benefit from this text. It is important to understand this.

If you read about this commandment, understand, and practice it, I am sure it will improve both your professional and personal life. I'm also sure that all of us realize that our careers and personal lives are closely interrelated and that problems in either one usually affect the other. If you are not happy with your career, you are very likely to take it out on the people in your life you love most. You are also very likely to bring your personal problems to work with you and to take them out on your students. After all, teachers are human, too. The best classrooms are a mix of sound subject matter, effective classroom management, and a superior attitude on the part of the teacher. Whether we like it or not, our students learn more from *how we act* than from *what we teach*. Our attitude and behavior show every day; the classroom is our stage and we have a captive audience. We not only lead by example, we *teach* by example. In my 20 years as a parent, manager, consultant, coach and as a teacher, I have found that attitudes have universal application. In order to "make that change," as the Michael Jackson song says, you may need to review the message of this chapter periodically. But I am sure that when the message clicks, it will change your life for the better.

By this point in our lives, our attitude has become an integral part of our personality. Any of the people in our lives who deal with us on a regular basis can provide a fairly accurate assessment of our attitudes. We can do the same for family members, friends, and acquaintances. It takes a *conscious* effort to improve or change an attitude. It is important to realize, however, that there is good reason to become introspective and evaluate ourselves in this regard. My experience has proven to me that the common thread in virtually all successful people is a positive attitude. Surely if success is the reward, then each of us can benefit greatly from an attitude adjustment.

You will remember that the Fourth Commandment suggests that you should "Dangle the Carrot High." Most teachers are familiar with the basis of this commandment. According to the Pygmalion effect, or self-fulfilling prophecy, people (students, in this case) will function at the level of our expectations. Our expectations, unfortunately, are often tainted by our prejudices, misconceptions, or attitudes. Let me give you an example of how attitudes can dictate events.

My former employer, the Internal Revenue Service, hired thousands of employees annually. One particularly crucial job required typing skills. Before prospective employees could take the typing examination, however, they had to take a written examination. Those who passed the written examination, but failed to meet the minimum typing requirements were often referred to as DDE (Direct Data Entry) flunkees or failees. For years, this label had an extremely negative effect on the employees as well as the organization. Because these applicants did not meet the typing speed and accuracy requirements but had scored high enough on the written test to be hired, the organization was obligated to place them in entry-level positions due to a collective bargaining agreement. The problem was that nobody wanted anything to do with them. Some managers fought to escape being

43

stuck with the dreaded flunkees. The irony was that the only shortcoming of these people was their inability to pass the typing test. Many of them actually scored higher on the written test than others who had been hired as typists. The myth continued for years until one segment of the organization requested some flunkees. The managers in this department pointed out that the previous year they had hired flunkees who had been very conscientious and hard-working employees. How could this be?

The managers realized that these people were good, solid employees whose only problem was that over the years the stereotypical label flunkees had become reality. Once managers learned that DDE flunkees was a misnomer and that these employees were productive, the stigma was lessened considerably.

The applications for educators are obvious. Many of us consciously or subconsciously have some of these same negative attitudes toward certain students. When we possess such attitudes, we become a major part of the problem. For example, stereotypes exist about Southeast Asian immigrants, Hispanics, African-Americans, and women. Some are so ingrained that we may not even be aware we have them. It is important to be openminded enough to face these stereotypes head-on and deal with them. Sensitivity and understanding can help to prevent lowering expectations and to avoid perpetuating such ethnic and sex stereotypes.

As an additional example—most of us have been conditioned to remember the negative and often downplay or forget the positive. When speaking to groups I often ask, "How many of you always seem to get into the 'wrong' (slowest moving) line at the supermarket?" Almost every hand goes up. I used to feel the same way until I decided to get scientific and keep track of the number of times I actually chose the wrong line. In fact, I picked the right line 80 percent of the time. Why did I feel that I picked the wrong line so often? Because I think most of us remember the one time we had to wait, and take the positive for granted. Again, we have been conditioned to accentuate the negative and we allow ourselves to distort the facts.

For the past six years I have spent a great deal of time observing people, their attitudes, and the effect attitudes have on our lives. I watch my children, my students, my wife, myself, people in the bank, the store, and other public places. There is a limitless amount of human interaction to observe if you want to learn about the impact of attitudes. The study of people and their attitudes is, in my opinion, the most fascinating subject in the world.

My definition of attitude is: *our outlook toward life in general, and toward people and events in our life, in particular.* Attitudes can be classified as either good or bad. Most of us are drawn to people with good (positive) attitudes and repelled by people with bad (negative) attitudes. We may not realize our attraction to people with good attitudes—it is often an unconscious phenomenon. Ask yourself, "Who are the people I enjoy being around?" And conversely, "Who are the people I feel uncomfortable around?" Most of us will find our choice of acquaintances is based largely on their attitudes. Few people enjoy the company of a person with a negative attitude. What I hope to convince you of in the following pages is that *to a great extent, our attitudes dictate outcomes* (successes and failures).

How important is attitude? The Bakersfield (California) School District once surveyed employers in the community to rate a long list of employability skills, from most important to least important. Included were 10-key adding machine, typing, shorthand, bookkeeping, filing, and communication skills. Survey results showed that 97 percent of the employers felt that *dependability* and *attitude* were the most important traits for new employees. Attitude was defined as cooperation, willingness to learn, and working well with coworkers and customers.

In another study, the University of Michigan contacted employers of graduates to ask them what was the most accurate indicator of success on the job. In this case, the employers felt that job success was due to attitude (85 percent) and skills (15 percent).

If attitude is so important, why don't we see more people changing their attitudes? Why are so many of us reluctant to modify or improve this critical aspect of our lives? Don't we realize the tremendous impact it would have on our lives? I suppose that part of the answer is the fact that so many of us are set in our ways that we find changing our attitude very difficult. And since changing our attitude involves changing behavior, we are absolutely right. For human beings, behavior modification is a great challenge. The other reason we probably don't change behavior is that many of us do not realize that we need to improve our attitude. Stop for a moment and spend a few minutes reflecting on how you deal with your family, coworkers, friends, and other people you come in contact with. Are you satisfied with the way you handle yourself in these relationships? If not, you're perfectly normal. If you decide to do something to improve those relationships, you'll be anything but normal. You'll be exceptional.

Changing your attitude for the better will be a significant event in your life. Your friends, family, and significant others will begin to notice the difference in your attitude (although they won't be able to pinpoint *what* has changed). These people in your life will win in their dealings with you. They will find you more reasonable, more enthusiastic, more patient, more fun to be around, and a good person to talk to. That is why *when the people in your life win, you win.*

Don't have any grand illusions about how to go about changing your attitude. It can be accomplished only through mental awareness and hard work, and *more hard work and self-critiquing.* Behavioral scientists know that it is extremely difficult for humans to modify their behavior.

46

In my 11 years of management experience, I had to change my style of dealing with people considerably in order to remain effective. Often this required swallowing my pride. There were times when I couldn't swallow my pride and lost my objectivity. Almost always this came back to haunt me. Too often many people make the same mistake, fighting the obvious rather than changing their behavior in order to keep focused on the goal.

As I mentioned in the Eighth Commandment, the ability to recognize changes in society and in people puts you on the cutting edge of your profession, whatever it may be. *Time* magazine recently reported a 1990 survey indicating that only 30 percent of people under 30 had "read a newspaper yesterday" ("The Tuned-Out Generation," July 9, 1990). According to the article, a Gallup poll in 1965 found that 67 percent of the same age group said they had "read a newspaper yesterday." Does this statistic impact educators? It certainly does. What we do with such information says a great deal about how seriously we take our job and how effectively perform. But it also illustrates the importance of modifying our behavior(s) in order to maintain our focus of delivering an education to students. In any discussion about attitude, motivation is the key concept. The word *motivation* has Greek roots and means to *move self.* Taken at face value some might say that if the origin of the word is accurate, then learning to succeed must come from within each student. While this certainly might be true, teachers, managers, parents, and others in a leadership role surely cannot underestimate their ability to create an environment where people want to produce, excel, or, in the school's case, want to learn. In a sense, teachers are able to spark the desire (motivation) to learn. This is the power of teaching. Experienced teachers may not have been told so, but they certainly know they have significantly affected the lives of some of their students. Inspiring others is one of the most rewarding of all accomplishments. It takes a special talent to have this kind of impact on others.

We have discussed how difficult it is to change the behavior of adults, let alone students. As so-called rational creatures, we often let hidden agendas take our focus off our goals. In addition, I believe that we are bombarded with negativism to such an extent that we underestimate how much it influences our lives. For example, I once worked with an individual who always left me with an uncomfortable feeling. I had known him for years and we usually only exchanged pleasantries. It wasn't until I became interested in studying attitudes and their substantial impact on outcomes that I realized what made me feel uneasy about him. This person was unbelievably negative. He viewed life through a cynic's glasses. When I would pass by and ask him how he was doing, he would scowl, "waiting until 4 o'clock, Friday"—an obvious commentary on his feelings about his job. I now realize that his look-at-the-darkside approach to life was very deenergizing. I can remember walking away from many of these assaults of negativism wondering how miserable he must have been. Yet, each of us probably knows at least one person like him. For example, a high school student made this interesting comment: "If a teacher hates his job so much, why doesn't he quit and do something else?" When I pressed the student as to how he knew the teacher "hated his job", the student's response was straightforward. "You can tell by his attitude toward the students, Mr. Reyes."

How do we overcome such negativism? It's a difficult task to tackle because, as I mentioned earlier, it is widespread. Take Blue Mondays, for example. Listen to people on Monday making themselves miserable talking about how terrible it is to be starting a new work or school week. Why are so many of us unwilling to look at the beginning of the work week in more positive terms?

Then there is the "best" day of the week—TGIF (Thank God, it's Friday!).

Negative bumper stickers and desk signs, too, are so common that we subconsciously have come to accept them as normal. "The boss may not always be right, but he's always the boss." "Don't tell me what kind of day to have!" The list seems endless. There is nothing "normal" about negativism, but it is so commonplace we don't realize how much it affects us.

Too often, students in my first-period class say, "Mr. Reyes, today is just a bad day." My reply is, "Wait a minute, this is first period and you're already predicting a bad day? If you have a bad day today, it will be because you decided to have one when you woke up this morning."

Consequently, the deeper the negativism runs, the more cynical we become, and ultimately the more self-centered and selfish we behave. We begin to think we're more important than we really are. To counteract any tendencies in this direction, I remember the advice of a speaker I heard several years ago: "If you think you're so important, remember this: The number of people at your funeral will depend on the weather."

This tendency toward negativism that pervades our lives often manifests itself in something called "ego-popping." This theory describes humans as creatures who walk around carrying balloons that represent their egos. Some of us have little balloons; some have *very large* balloons. Because many of us are subconsciously negative, we have the habit of "popping" other people's balloons. When we deflate another's ego, our express intent is to make that person feel bad, although many times we don't realize it. When we make people feel bad, *they lose. When they lose, we lose.* Telling someone he burnt the toast (he saw the smoke billowing out of the toaster, too!) or that her room looks like a pigpen (even if it *does*) serves little useful purpose and tends only to escalate hostilities.

Without realizing it, many of us can become fairly good ego-poppers. My daughter could have been a professional milk spiller. She was good at it, and consistent, too. We could count on her spilling her milk at least once a week. She would also make some of the biggest messes imaginable. Her glasses of milk would usually fall to the floor and explode all over the kitchen. In most cases, children feel guilty enough without their parents berating them for something they did accidentally. I used to get angry at my daughter, but she did it so often I probably learned the hard way that patience really is a virtue. It reached the point that the family could laugh about it. "Angelica spilled her milk? Yes, I guess it's about that time." As soon as I learned to accept these accidents for what they were (unintentional messy little inconveniences), a funny thing happened. She no longer spilled her milk.

I must confess I am a reformed pessimist. I used to be cynical. In high school I played quarterback on the football team. Once before a practice game an assistant coach came over to me while I was dressing and told me that the first play would be a pass. After the coach walked away I pretended to be a play-by-play announcer. To one of my teammates nearby I blurted out, "Reyes back to pass . . . he looks, he throws . . . it's intercepted!" When the game started I went back to pass. I looked. I threw and. . . it *was* intercepted! As a teenager I shrugged it off, but the irony was still evident to me. I didn't realize it at the time but I would later be greatly influenced by this event. It was an example of fulfilling a self-declared prophecy. When I began studying the effects of attitudes on our lives, I vividly recalled those events of my junior year in high school. But what I began to realize was the great potential of *positive* self-declarations. Clearly, optimism has much greater benefits than does pessimism.

All this leads us back to the original premise—that negativism leads to negative results. Positivism leads to positive results. And since it always starts with people, there is an important message here for all of us who want to deal with people more effectively. *Build people (students) up, don't tear them down.* I'm talking about your students, your spouses, your children—all the people you come in contact with. There are no benefits from tearing people down. At a school district in-service session I conducted, a teacher shared this saying with me: "Burning your neighbor's house down doesn't make your house look any better." I believe that all my experiences of the past 20 years have given me an understanding of the critical role attitude plays in determining successes and shortcomings.

Because I am a student of human nature, I can tell you—without a moment's hesitation—that observing, interacting, and studying humans and their behavior, for me, is the most fascinating subject in the world. I spend a good part of each day making mental notes about the people with whom I come in contact. What is their outlook on life? How do they treat other people? How do people react when treated in a negative manner? How do they respond to compliments or positive reinforcement? My children, I have noticed, have picked up my interest in attitudes and behavior. After seeing the movie, *Teenwolf,* for example, they excitedly told me how teenwolf's basketball teammates had negative attitudes. They were referring to the scene in which the teenwolf decides that all the notoriety he receives when he transforms himself into the werewolf is not worth it. As a werewolf, however, he has tremendous basketball skills that he uses to lead his team to the championship game. When he arrives at the game as a normal person, his teammates, accustomed to playing with the dominant werewolf, automatically assume they will lose the game. I was impressed that my children noticed this defeatist attitude. Recognizing a shortcoming is the first step in the improvement process. Developing a negative approach to life is the easy out. Developing a positive outlook requires hard work and conscious effort. Because negativism abounds in our lives, it takes special people to catch themselves before they spread a little gloom into another person's life.

Everyone has responsibilities, frustrations, and disappointments. One of my sons was suspended from school for three days. When my boys were young they picked all the grapefruit from a neighbor's only tree and squashed them in the street. They also threw dirt rocks into another neighbor's pool. For many parents, these are probably familiar scenarios. As children get older, the stakes grow larger. Drugs, alcohol, pregnancies, and other real-life issues become reality for parents. We must learn to deal with these situations, providing discipline and love in appropriate doses. On the other hand, we cannot let these adversities control our lives or, more importantly, our outlook or attitude about life. Yes, we can become angry, frustrated, annoyed, and depressed. But should we dwell on the negative or keep moving forward and make something good happen by stressing the bright side?

In the classroom, I think teachers need to be Academy Award winners. In other words, we should always portray a positive attitude, *especially when we don't feel like it.* To be sure, this takes some conscious mental effort and discipline because we all have personal trials and tribulations. If we take these problems out on our students or our family members, how professionally are we acting? Most of us do this more often than we would like to admit. Remember, our faces don't lie and children pick up on this quickly.

Adults and children need *consistency* in their relationships. We need to feel comfortable that we can predict the reaction of our boss, teacher, or parent in our dealings with them. Whenever someone in our lives flies off the handle one time and not the next, it is frustrating for us. When we, as teachers, let things bother us, we run the risk of managing our classrooms *inconsistently.*

We need to practice what we preach. It is unfortunate that students quickly learn not to "bother" their teachers because they are in a bad mood. When students have to tread carefully through our classrooms, we are not leading by example. How many times do we, as teachers, tell our students, "Don't get discouraged. Don't let little things bother you. Keep your head up!" When we come to class in a less-than-positive mood, expect your students to do the same. Remember, to many students you are a role model and the most influential person in their lives. Live up to it!

Once we make a real commitment to improving our attitude, we begin seeing immediate results. You will find yourself making positives out of negatives. You won't let irritations gnaw at you as much. Your cup will be half-full more often than it will be half-empty. You'll be better able to find the silver lining in the dark clouds of life.

Because changing our attitudes requires a conscious effort on our part, it is a mental process. And it is good to remember that the mind is a very powerful tool. If we choose to fill it with cynicism, negative thoughts, and pessimism, it will direct our lives in that direction. On the other hand, if we downplay the negative, refuse to dwell on our adversities, and actively accentuate and perform positive actions, our lives will take another, very different path.

How powerful is the mind? Here is a simple example. One hot summer night my 10-year-old son woke up claiming to have been bitten by mosquitoes. He was scratching his legs and said he couldn't go to sleep. I told him to wash himself off with a cool washcloth and to go back to sleep. He washed and went back to bed only to get up again, claiming his legs still itched. I told him to get up so I could put some "mosquito bite medicine" on him. After this, he went to bed, fell asleep promptly and had no further problems. What he didn't know was that the medicine I applied was suntan lotion. In my son's mind, however, he had just received something to soothe his bites. Once he convinced himself that his misery was about to be relieved, he fell asleep. This is a modest case of mind over matter. Many of you I'm sure can relate similar experiences.

Most people like to think that they are open-minded, can take an issue or event, analyze it, and intellectually draw some kind of objective conclusion. For most of us, however, it is probably more accurate to say that we base such conclusions on emotion, our first impression, on how we initially react. This is not what the Greek philosophers had in mind when they said that humans are rationally thinking creatures.

On the other hand, it is this reactive nature that makes us unique and fun to interact with. Earlier I talked about using "off-the-wall" behavior to get the attention of students. Such behavior plays into the hands of the reactive nature of humans. It is unexpected, attention-getting behavior that makes students and other people focus on you. Once you have someone's attention, you have generated interest. And once you have that interest, it's a matter of delivering your message. Mix that with discipline, "Dangling the Carrot High," "Erasing All Question Marks," precise communication, an enthusiastic approach, and you have created a learning environment in which it would be difficult not to be excellent. One of the major purposes of the Tenth Commandment is to help you become conscious of the effect of negative attitudes on our lives. Correspondingly, positive attitudes and behavior have a converse effect on our careers and our personal lives. *In the classroom and in life we must reinforce positive behavior in order to perpetuate it.*

To avoid misinterpretation of my message about positive attitudes and behavior, I should point out that there is a time and place to be firm with students who are considerably less cooperative than they should be. I once heard a remarkably accurate description of people: 80 percent of the people in the world are easy to work with, 19 percent are difficult to work with, and 1 percent are impossible to work with. The teacher's golden rule should read: Don't let the "one percenters" ruin it for you and the other 99 percent. How many times have teachers seen regulations, rules, or policies established to combat the one percenters? The obvious problem here is that we punish, or at least confine, the 99 percent because of the behavior of the few. This is the most common way we let the one percenters ruin it for us. Do we ever let a few students get under our skin and then take out our irritation on the others? This is something to consider carefully.

A great benefit of not allowing one percenters to dominate is that you learn to control situations they would normally control. You'll find yourself deflecting the anger you might have ordinarily felt to the person who is creating the undesirable situation.

Take, for example, the all-too-common statement, "He (or she) made me mad!" This, of course, is an inaccurate remark. *No one* can make another person mad without that person's permission. Yes, events can trigger emotions. But anger can and will be controlled when you decide to control it. Anger is an *emotion*. Emotions are internally generated. In many cases the person who "made you mad" is enjoying his/her accomplishment. If you react in the opposite manner (not getting mad), often the other person will get mad because of your unexpected reaction. Thus, you can control the situation.

Perhaps the most significant trait of people with superior attitudes is their ability to cope with adversity. Many people cannot deal with failure. They give in; they quit. But if you study people who are successful, you will find that most of them fail more often than the average person. That is because the only person who doesn't make mistakes is the person who doesn't try anything.

All of us know or have observed individuals with tremendous resiliency, the ability to be stronger, more determined in the face of adversity. They possess such traits because of their extraordinary attitudes. For example, Rod Perry became a coach for the Seattle Seahawks. At 5'8", 180 pounds, he was one of the smallest players in professional football. During his senior year in high school he suffered severe knee ligament damage. Recounting this event with one of my high school classes one day, he told the students that his doctor told him his football playing days were over. When a student asked Rod how he felt about this news, Rod responded, "I knew that no one except the good Lord and myself can tell me what I can or cannot do." Even though I had known Rod for 20 years I learned something about him that perhaps I had underestimated. His attitude, his will to succeed, and his determination were his most significant personal assets and probably were the main reason for his success in his professional and personal life.

Terry Fox, whose leg was amputated due to cancer, decided to run across the nation to raise money for cancer research. Many people thought he was crazy, but everyone was touched by his courage, his determination, his inspiration for us all. Terry Fox had a superior, never-say-die attitude. Remarkably, he raised $13 million for cancer research before his death. He was truly an inspirational human being.

Bill Demby has two artificial legs. Most of us have seen him doing television commercials. Despite his combat injuries, he lives an astoundingly normal life. He can play basketball with his friends due not only to today's technology, but mostly to his positive attitude. He decided long ago that he wouldn't use his handicap as an excuse for not developing to his full potential. His message is clear: Handicapped people are no less human than any other individuals, so don't expect less from them or pity them.

At the time of this writing Hulda Crooks was 91-years-young. She maintains her hobby of mountain climbing, recently completing a climb of one of Japan's highest peaks. Ms. Crooks isn't fazed a bit by her feats or her age. In an interview following her latest climb, she announced her plans to continue climbing as long as she continues to feel fit.

Again, the common thread among all these unique individuals is their attitude. Their ability to do what others told them they couldn't do makes them refreshingly rare. They are unswayed by the limitations others place on their potential. They are extremely confident in their resolve to reach their goals. And, perhaps most importantly, they don't let anything get in their way. As the saying goes, "Obstacles are what you see when you take your eyes off the goal."

This last attribute, this stick-to-itiveness despite stumbling blocks, is the real test of attitude. Anyone can be enthusiastic, energetic, and positive when things are going well. But how many of us are able to maintain our spirit, remain upbeat, stay focused, not make excuses or become testy when adversity knocks us off course? How many of us can keep our best foot forward and do our best despite a series of setbacks? How many have the confidence that rarely waivers, regardless of the attitudes of cynics?

A special person with whom I worked for a number of years serves as a source of inspiration for me. Cruz Garza worked with me while I was employed by the government. In the early 1970s she lost a son in an automobile accident. Seven years later lighting struck again. She lost a second son in a traffic accident. And, unbelievably, seven years later she lost a third son in a construction accident. Only someone who has had a similar experience could begin to understand what Cruz Garza has been through. It has been a burden of nightmarish proportions; yet, in my contacts with her, I never heard her dwell on it, never saw it affect her dealings with her employees, and never saw her use it as an excuse in any way. Every time I think something might be going wrong, I think about this remarkable woman and say to myself, "If Cruz Garza could deal with her adversity in such a positive manner, certainly I can deal with my small problems."

It is appropriate to close with a discussion of the goal-setting process. I can't think of any individual I consider successful who is *not* goal-oriented. On the other hand, I know people who are goal-oriented, who never seem to realize their dreams. Why is this?

The process of goal setting and goal realization is probably one of the most vivid examples of the power of positive thinking. It begins with the mental visualization of a desired state (goal). When I decided to change careers I mentally visualized (dreaming is another, often misunderstood, word for the same process) myself in front of the classroom, teaching students. From that mental visualization came the actual goal: to be a teacher. I gave myself a timetable. I was 32-years-old at the time, and I wanted to finish the required course work and to start teaching before my 36th birthday. When I began teaching, I was 35-years-old.

Goals are almost always the result of mental visualization of a desired state. We may dream of being an administrator, of having a master's degree, of being 30 pounds lighter. We desire a multitude of things in our lives. Some goals may be related to careers, others to family, and others may be personal goals such as quitting or cutting back on smoking. We might want to improve relationships with friends or family members. All these life improvements begin with visualizing ourselves as we want to be. Very few major or minor improvements in life happen by accident. They are the result of well-thought-out, well-conceived, and well-executed plans.

Some people find it helpful to write their goals on paper. Whether you do this or not is an individual judgment. I write some goals (mostly long-range goals), but most of them are firmly implanted in my mind. Regardless of what you choose to do, always remember that goals *give your life direction.* They provide you with a sense of purpose and a focus.

A simple equation to follow in goal setting is:

$$YOU + MOTIVATION = SUCCESS$$

Motivation can be broken up into three components: goals, hard work, and enthusiasm. As mentioned earlier, goals are the critical part of this improvement process. We should also remember to establish goals of a moderate degree of risk. People who set goals that are unrealistic or only remotely attainable will rarely, if ever, reach them and will ultimately give up on the goal-setting process itself. Accomplishing goals is energizing and leads to the establishment of additional, more challenging goals. Therefore, establish your initial goals at a level you are confident you can achieve.

Hard work is necessary to accomplish anything we desire. *There is no substitute for hard work!* One of the most appropriate sayings I ever came across reads: "The harder I work, the luckier I get." I have found this to be true.

Lastly, remember Ralph Waldo Emerson's advice: "Nothing great was ever accomplished without enthusiasm." Think about an enthusiastic person you know. What kind of influence does this person have on others? Do you notice less complaining or excuse making from this person? Why? Almost always, success and enthusiasm go hand in hand.

People with positive attitudes have a special edge. It makes them unique in a positive way. It can make you exceptional in all your endeavors and an inspiration to others—a reputation anyone could be proud of.

According to an old saying,

There are three kinds of people:
Those who make things happen,
those who watch things happen,
and those who wonder what happened.

People with positive attitudes *make things happen.*

If this text helps you improve your personal life, I will be very happy. If it helps you improve your teaching skills, I'll be even happier. You will probably find out that these two improvements are mutually inclusive—improvement in one area will almost automatically lead to improvement in the other. If this occurs I will say, "Mission accomplished!" You see, this publication is the realization of one of my goals. If it helps you become a better teacher, our students win.

AND IF OUR STUDENTS WIN, WE ALL WIN.

APPENDIX

COURSE EVALUATION

Course Name _____ Period _____

1. *Course Content:* Did you learn what you expected to learn from the course?

2. *Interest Level:* What did you like most about this course?

What did you like *least* about the course?

3. *Classroom Discipline:* In your opinion, do you feel that the classroom environment was conducive to learning? Were students disciplined in a fair manner?

4. *Teaching Methods:* Was the subject taught in an interesting manner? If not, what suggestions do you have for improving the way the course is taught?

5. *Explanation:* Were new lessons explained clearly? Were student questions answered in a way that students could understand? Did you feel you could ask a question anytime?

6. *Grading System:* Did you understand how your grade was determined? Did you always know where you stood? Did you feel the grading system was fair?

7. *Student/Teacher Communication:* Did you feel that you could ask your teacher questions, share a problem, etc.? Did you feel the teacher would give you extra help if you needed it?

8. Any other comments:

ACKNOWLEDGMENT

To my parents, Raymundo and Maria—for teaching me the value of a good education; to my children, Mario, Carlos, Angelica, and Melina—who are my most precious possessions; to my wife, Esther—for those four miracles of life and for understanding when I chose to sacrifice the "big bucks" for my passion to teach; to my students at Parlier High School—for proving all those people wrong who told me I made a mistake by becoming a teacher—I look forward to every class period; to my varsity football players—for calling me "Mr. Reyes," not "Coach," as soon as football season is over, showing that you consider me a teacher first; to all teachers—*never* forget, you really can make a difference.